DATE DUE

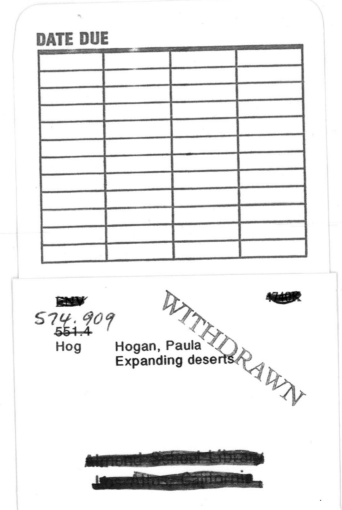

Expanding DESERTS

BY PAULA HOGAN

ENVIRONMENT ALERT!

Gareth Stevens Children's Books
MILWAUKEE

For a free color catalog describing Gareth Stevens' list of high-quality children's books, call 1-800-341-3569 (USA) or 1-800-461-9120 (Canada).

Library of Congress Cataloging-in-Publication Data

Hogan, Paula Z.
    Expanding deserts / Paula Hogan.
      p. cm. — (Environment alert)
    Includes bibliographical references and index.
    Summary: Discusses the causes of desertification, its consequences, and what can be done to stop the spread of deserts.
    ISBN 0-8368-0474-0
    1. Desertification—Juvenile literature. [1. Desertification.] I. Title. II. Series.
GB611.H64 1991
551.4'15—dc20   90-27799

A Gareth Stevens Children's Books edition

Edited, designed, and produced by
Gareth Stevens Children's Books
1555 North RiverCenter Drive, Suite 201
Milwaukee, Wisconsin 53212, USA

Picture Credits
From the American Geographical Society Collection, University of Wisconsin-Milwaukee Library, pp. 10 (lower left), 16; Courtesy of the Arizona-Sonora Desert Museum, pp. 2-3, 4, 25 (upper); Gareth Stevens, Inc., © 1991, pp. 6-7 (line art), 10 (upper), 21 (upper); CARE PHOTO by Michael Ahearn, p. 17 (lower); CARE PHOTO by Tom Sheffel, p. 17 (upper left); Ted H. Funk/Third Coast, © 1988, p. 26 (lower); Matthew Groshek, © 1991, pp. 28-29; Grant Heilman/Grant Heilman Photography, p. 19 (inset); Historical Pictures Service, Inc., p. 9 (lower right); Rick Karpinski/DeWalt & Associates, pp. 6-7 (illustration), 18-19; Regis Lefebure/Third Coast, © 1990, p. 5; Larry Lefever from Grant Heilman, p. 24 (upper); © Steve McCurry/Magnum Photos, front cover (inset); Mark Mille/DeWalt & Associates, pp. 12-13, 22-23; Pat Ortega, pp. 26-27; Alan Pitcairn from Grant Heilman, pp. 24-25; TASS from SOVFOTO, pp. 20 (both), 21 (lower); UNICEF/Maggie Murray-Lee, pp. 14, 23 (lower); UNICEF/Maria Antonietta Peru, p. 15; UNICEF/Carolyn Watson, p. 22 (lower); Frank Zullo, © 1982, p. 27 (lower).

Series editors: Kelli Peduzzi and Patricia Lantier-Sampon
Series designer: Laurie Shock
Picture researcher: Daniel Helminak
Assistant picture researcher: Diane Laska
Research editor: Jamie Daniel
Editorial assistant: Scott Enk

Printed in the United States of America

2 3 4 5 6 7 8 9 97 96 95 94 93

At this time, Gareth Stevens, Inc., does not use 100 percent recycled paper, although the paper used in our books does contain about 30 percent recycled fiber. This decision was made after a careful study of current recycling procedures revealed their dubious environmental benefits. We will continue to explore recycling options.

Production Director   President

CONTENTS

Deserts on the March 4
Deserts around the World.............................6
The Desert Begins to Spread 8
The Edge of the Desert 10
Fact File — The Sahel: A Way of Life Destroyed....12

Holding Back the Desert 16
Saving the Trees 16
Keeping the Soil in Place 18
Fact File — The Shrinking Aral Sea......................20
Saving Precious Water 22

Natural Deserts in Danger 26

Research Activities...28
Things You Can Do to Help 30
Places to Write for More Information 30
More Books to Read 30
Glossary 31
Index 32

DESERTS ON THE MARCH

Deserts are the driest places on Earth. They receive less than ten inches (25.4 cm) of rain each year. Deserts may get no rain at all for many years. People often think of deserts as sandy places. But most desert land is rocky and covered with pebbles. Deserts are also some of the hottest places on Earth. Temperatures may reach 131°F (55°C) during the daytime. The desert is home to many animals and plants that have learned to survive in this harsh habitat.

Unfortunately, deserts in many areas of the world are spreading. Long **droughts** have set in. People misuse the farmland at the edge of the desert, which turns to bare, dry **wasteland**. Nothing will ever survive in these wastelands, not even plants and animals that live in the natural desert. Scientists call this "**desertification**," even though the land isn't turning into a natural desert. They use the word *desertification* to mean the process by which land becomes unable to support life. If people don't stop turning the land into wasteland, much of life on Earth will not survive.

Above: Many kinds of plants can live in the hot, dry desert. The tall, spiky saguaro (sa-WAH-row) cactus lives in the Sonoran Desert of Arizona. It can store up to seven tons of water in its thick stem!

Opposite: The desert in Monument Valley, Arizona, has unusual rock formations that were formed by wind and water erosion.

North America

Deserts around the World

South America

Huge natural deserts exist all over the world, but not all of them are alike. Most are caused by dry winds that blow over the land. Other deserts are cool and foggy, such as deserts on the sea-coast. Two large deserts — at the North and South poles — are the coldest places on Earth. These deserts get less than four inches (10 cm) of snowfall each year. Since this moisture is frozen, it cannot be used by plants and animals.

Asia

Africa

Australia

Antarctica

The Desert Begins to Spread

At the edge of the natural desert are grasslands where people live and grow crops. But too many people live there, and they damage this land. They cut down all the trees for firewood. Their cows, goats, and sheep eat so much grass that it cannot grow back. The trampling hooves of their animals pack down the earth so that no seeds can sprout.

Wind and rain can also damage the land. The wind picks up the fertile **topsoil** and blows it away. Soil that was once held in place by plant roots is washed away by the rain. This process is called **erosion**, and it changes the land forever. Once the topsoil disappears, it cannot be replaced.

Deserts spread in patches. The topsoil in several small areas disappears. Then, the patches of erosion enlarge and grow together into acres of wasteland where nothing can live. In this way, 15 million acres (6 million ha) of useful land are desertified each year.

Upper left: An area in Mali, one of six countries in the Sahel region of Africa, was fertile land before desertification set in.

Lower left: The same area after desertification. Desertification has many causes. One big cause is the planting of crops that damage the soil. In the 1960s, some Sahelian governments made farmers plant too many fields of cotton and peanuts to sell for cash. These crops soon wore out the soil.

The Dust Bowl

Drought also desertifies the land. In the 1930s, a long drought turned parts of the Great Plains of North America into the "Dust Bowl." The topsoil blew away in terrible dust storms, and nothing could grow.

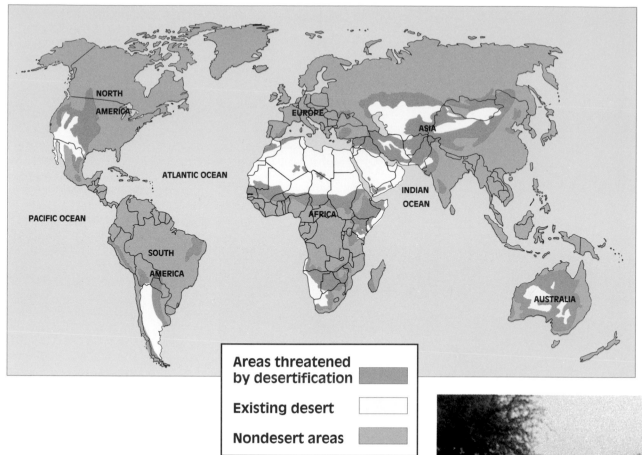

Areas threatened by desertification	(dark gray)
Existing desert	(white)
Nondesert areas	(light gray)

The Edge of the Desert

Usually, the land near the edge of the desert gets about twice as much rain as the desert itself. Yet water is still scarce. Only grass, scattered trees, and shrubs will grow there. Farmers plow small areas of these grasslands. They must plant crops that need little water to grow.

In the Middle East and parts of Africa, the peoples living in the lands near the desert are called **nomads**. They herd cows, goats, or sheep from place to place. Nomads follow the rains in search of grass and water for their herds.

Opposite, upper: Areas on the edges of many natural deserts are becoming desertified.

Opposite, lower: Land near the edge of this desert in Tunisia is green, but dry. If the land is mistreated, or if drought sets in, the area may quickly become desertified.

Below: Nomadic herders in Mali lead their cattle across dry land as they search for water and more fertile pastures.

Fact File
The Sahel: A Way of Life Destroyed

In the Sahel, an area stretching across six nations in northern Africa, almost no rain has fallen in over 20 years! This drought has desertified the land and destroyed people's lives.

In the 1960s, rain fell more heavily than usual — as much as 20 inches (50.8 cm) in good years. More grass grew, so nomads let their herds grow larger. The nomads also dug wells to water the herds.

Opposite: The Sahel stretches across the country of Mali, where much grazing land has turned to desert.

Below: Many green areas are gradually becoming desertified because of tree cutting and overgrazing. Drought also speeds up the process. This artist's rendering shows how a patch of land looks before and after it is desertified.

Then the drought struck, drying up the rivers. Cattle crowded around the new wells, trampling the ground and eating all the plants. Little by little, the land became bare. Blowing sand replaced the topsoil. Millions of people and cattle starved, and many died.

Cash-crop farming has also desertified the Sahel. In the past, farmers planted only enough to feed their families. But during the heavy rains, they planted huge crops of cotton and peanuts to sell. These crops quickly used up all the **nutrients** in the soil and made the fields useless. When the farmers abandoned their land, the topsoil blew away.

Because of drought and desertification, over 100,000 people have starved to death in the Sahel. The peoples of the Sahel have lost their way of life, and their land will never again be able to support them. But a tragedy of this size could have been prevented.

Opposite: Hungry children in a refugee camp wait hopefully for food.

Below: Because of drought and desertification, people who once lived on open grasslands or on small farms must crowd into refugee camps like this one in Chad.

HOLDING BACK THE DESERT

Saving the Trees

To stop deserts from spreading, we must first understand how land is desertified. This begins with the cutting of trees. Trees act as **windbreaks** to keep topsoil from blowing away. Tree roots also hold the soil in place, slowing erosion from wind and rain.

Below: These women in India have cut firewood to sell at the market. The cutting of trees for fuel speeds up desertification.

People cut down the trees for firewood or to clear farmland. Soon, no trees are left to shade the ground or hold the soil in place. The soil blows away, leaving a barren land. To stop desertification, the people of Ethiopia are planting trees that can grow with little water. In Niger, people have planted a windbreak of trees 230 miles (370 km) long! To slow the cutting of firewood, the United Nations gives out small stoves that use much less wood than cooking over an open fire.

From Forests to Deserts

Only 70 years ago, forests covered parts of India, Somalia, and Uganda. Farmers cleared the forests for planting. After only two harvests, nutrients in the soil were used up. The people moved on to clear new fields. Soon, thousands of forested acres turned into desert.

Left, top: This farmer from Nigeria plants a tree in his field. The tree's roots will help keep the topsoil in place, increasing the yield of his crops.

Left, bottom: Trees planted in double rows form windbreaks. They protect soil from wind erosion and improve harvests.

Keeping the Soil in Place

Desertification has set in when the topsoil has blown away, and nothing can grow. Tree cutting is only one way this happens. Drought, erosion, and **overgrazing** by animals are other causes. In times of drought, the grass dies. Overgrazing will also destroy the plant cover. Without plant roots to hold the soil in place, the wind blows the soil away. Erosion is made even worse when rain falls. Without plant roots to absorb water, the soil washes away, never to return.

The left side of this illustration shows that soil erodes when we mistreat the land (1). Heavy machinery chews up the ground (2). Deforestation (3) and overgrazing (4) imperil the topsoil. On the right side, we see that smaller animal herds (5) and terracing (6) are two ways to preserve the soil. Also, plants like the jojoba (7) do not need a lot of water to grow well in dry climates. Planting such crops is another way to use soil efficiently.

Many things can be done to keep the soil in place. In addition to planting trees, people can raise smaller animal herds. For instance, some ranchers in the United States have agreed to graze fewer cows on public lands. With fewer animals eating less grass, more plants will be left to hold the soil in place.

Contour plowing is another way to stop soil erosion. Instead of plowing in straight lines, farmers follow the dips and curves of the land. In Ethiopia and many other places, farmers have begun to contour-plow their fields. In such a field, the wind does not blow so much topsoil away. By keeping the topsoil in place, the land will be able to support plant and animal life.

The photograph below (inset) shows how contour plowing follows the natural curves of the land. This method of farming in hilly country helps water stay in the soil.

FACT FILE
The Shrinking Aral Sea

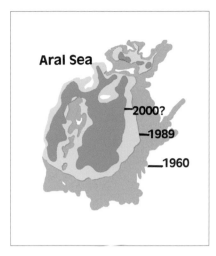

Aral Sea

2000?

1989

1960

Above: This map shows how the boundaries of the Aral Sea are steadily receding. The huge water losses in the past years have dramatically changed the lives of people who used to make their living by fishing in the sea. It seems likely that the size of the Aral Sea will continue to diminish.

Opposite, top: The Aral Sea is in the central Asian region of the Soviet Union. Its shores were once lined with thriving fishing villages.

Opposite, bottom: Today, the Aral Sea is drying up. Farmers are using the rivers that once filled the sea to irrigate crops in the desert. Without this river water, the sea is disappearing and leaving a bare, salty wasteland. The fishing villages are miles away from the water!

Right: Salty dust from the dry seabed makes many people sick. Children and old people suffer the most. This fisherman crouches near his useless boat. His son has never seen the sea near his home.

Two rivers flow into the Aral Sea, in the southwestern Soviet Union. For many years, farmers have taken water from these rivers to irrigate their cotton fields in the nearby desert. In fact, they have taken so much water that the Aral Sea is drying up! It has lost 11,000 square miles (28,500 sq km) of its surface area, or enough water to fill Lake Erie — twice! Fishing ports that used to be on the shore are now 20 miles (32 km) away from the water.

The land that used to be underwater has become a dusty salt flat. Salty dust blows over the cotton fields, killing the plants. The dust washes into wells, polluting the water. Wildlife has disappeared. Many people are sick or dying because they drink the polluted water and breathe the salty dust. The area around the Aral Sea has become a wasteland.

Saving Precious Water

To stop deserts from spreading, water must also be used carefully. In dry areas, water is scarce, and crops don't get enough rain. Farmers must **irrigate** their fields for their crops to survive. Unfortunately, the methods they use to water their crops can be wasteful. Almost half the water **evaporates** into the air before it ever reaches the plants!

Water is wasted when it seeps out of the irrigation ditches before it flows to the fields. The irrigation water also draws salt out of the soil. The salt forms a crust on the surface, and almost nothing can grow in it. Water pumped from deep under the ground irrigates many desert fields. But in some places, this underground water is being used up faster than it can be replaced, killing the natural desert plants. If water is wasted in this way, the area may become desertified.

Above: Some irrigation methods waste water. Most of the water in open irrigation ditches evaporates before it reaches the plants. Water pumped from deep underground may be used faster than it can be replaced.

Left: The government In Niger works with special international groups to provide the country's rural population with safe water.

Left: A Tuareg child from the Republic of Mali in Africa collects clean water from a hand pump.

The Drought-loving Jojoba

Farmers in dry areas are raising cash crops that need little water, such as **jojoba** (ho-HO-bah). Jojoba seed is a source of fine oil for **cosmetics** and industry.

Opposite (both): Drip-irrigation hoses and black plastic sheeting help keep crops moist without using a lot of water. Soon, delicious cantaloupes will grow in the field pictured in the top photograph; the California vineyard pictured at the bottom will produce crisp, juicy grapes.

Fortunately, farmers are using new ways to irrigate their crops that cut down on water waste. On large farms, pumps with built-in computers draw water from underground. The computer measures the dryness of the soil, and the pump sprays just the right amount of water on the crops. Less water is used, so less is wasted.

Drip irrigation cuts down on evaporation. A hose with tiny holes in it is placed close to the plant roots, and water slowly drips out. Almost all the water is absorbed by the roots. Very little evaporates into the air.

Heavy plastic sheeting at the base of plants helps the soil stay moist and keeps water-drinking weeds from growing. Another good way to save water is to grow crops that do well in dry climates.

NATURAL DESERTS IN DANGER

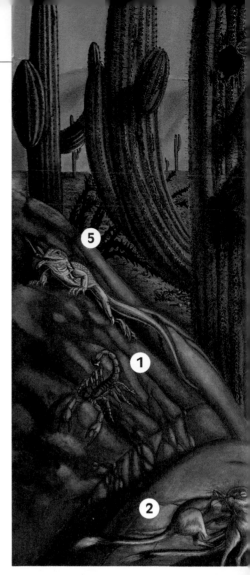

Many parts of the world are becoming desertified, but natural deserts are also in danger. Natural deserts, with their own special plant and animal **habitats**, are also in peril from human carelessness. Cities in the southwestern United States are growing and pushing into desert lands that once held only cacti and prairie dogs. Many desert areas are chewed up by dirt bikes that race across the fragile desert soil.

Another danger is the use of deserts as farmland, because plowing and irrigation destroy the natural habitat. In many deserts, gold, copper, and other precious minerals are mined, opening deep scars in the land. In the Nevada desert, nuclear bombs are exploded in underground tests.

Fortunately, many deserts in the North American west are being turned into national parks. By taking care of the natural deserts, these habitats will survive for a long time to come. And if we preserve the fragile lands at the desert's edge, they will continue to support life on Earth.

Right: An opal mine in New South Wales, Australia, leaves deep scars in the desert.

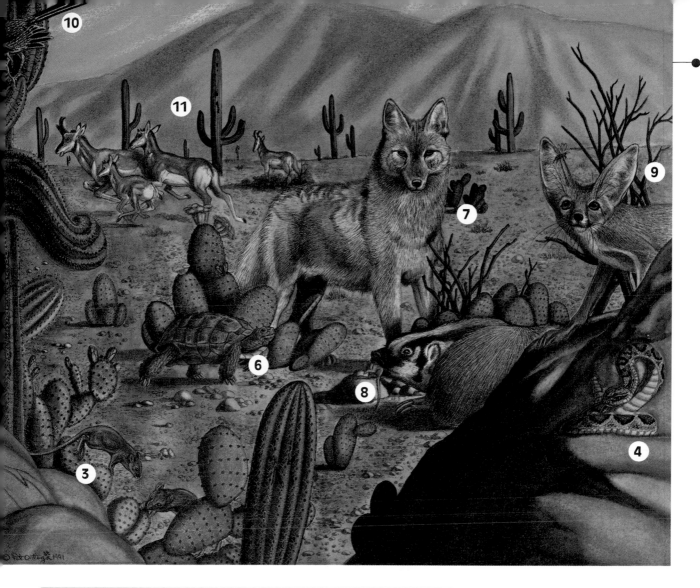

Above: The animals of the Sonoran Desert in the south-western U.S. are adapted to the harsh climate. Some are sandy in color, which keeps them cool by reflecting the Sun's rays. Bottom, left to right: scorpion (1), kangaroo rat (2), pocket mouse (3), diamondback rattlesnake (4). Middle, left to right: green collared lizard (5), desert tortoise (6), coyote (7), badger (8), desert fox (9). Top, left to right: crested lark (10), pronghorn antelope (11).

Left: Building the city of Phoenix, Arizona, destroyed the natural desert habitat.

27

RESEARCH ACTIVITIES

1. **Learn more about evaporation.**
   Cut a piece of wet cloth into three equal parts.
   Lay one flat in the Sun, lay one in the shade, and
   hang one in the Sun. Which one dries the
   fastest? Fill two saucers of the same size with
   water. Place one near a sunny window, the
   other in the refrigerator. After two days, what
   has happened to the water in each saucer?

2. **Discover how desert plants get moisture from
   sand that seems dry.**
   Dig a hole about two feet (61 cm) deep in
   sandy ground. (Ask an adult if it is safe to dig
   there first.) Place a cup in the center. Cover
   the hole with a plastic sheet, and fasten the edges
   down. Place a stone in the center of the sheet,
   over the cup. Watch as drops of water form on
   the underside of the sheet and fall into the cup.
   The Sun warmed the sand in the hole. Moisture
   that was held by the sand evaporated and
   condensed, or re-formed as water, on the
   plastic sheet.

3. Learn more about temperature.

Use a thermometer to measure the temperature at noon one day. What is the temperature in a sunny, treeless place? In a shady place? Near a pond or lake? In the basement? Compare the temperatures you find in these different environments.

4. Experiment with growing plants in different soils.

Fill one container with garden soil, another container with sand. Plant lettuce seeds in both containers, put them on a sunny windowsill, and water them gently every three or four days. Compare what happens to the seeds in the garden soil with what happens to the seeds in the "desert" soil.

Things You Can Do to Help

The following activities will help stop desertification. Try to involve your friends, family, and classmates in your conservation efforts.

1. Call your local water company and find out ways to save water. Make a list of these rules and post them in your home and classroom.

2. With your friends and classmates, organize a fund-raising event, such as a bake sale. Send the proceeds to CARE, 660 First Avenue, New York, New York 10016, and ask them to use the money to plant trees in the Sahel.

3. Write to your state, provincial, or national lawmakers, asking them to pass laws that protect the land from desertification.

Places to Write for More Information

The following organizations work to save the environment. When you write to them for more information, be specific about what you want to know.

Canadian Nature
   Federation
75 Albert Street,
   Suite 203
Ottawa, Ontario K1P 9Z9

Greenpeace USA
1436 U Street NW
Washington, D.C. 20009

The Wilderness Society
1400 I Street NW
Washington, D.C. 20005

More Books to Read

All About Deserts, by John Sanders (Troll)
Deserts and Wastelands, by Dougal Dixon (Watts)
Ecology: Learning to Love Our Planet, by Susan Diffenderfer (Zephyr)
Ecology Basics, by Lawrence Stevens (Prentice Hall)
Save the Earth! by Betty Miles (Knopf)

Glossary

contour plowing — turning over the soil following the curves of the land

cosmetics — substances used to make the body more attractive

desertification — the process by which land becomes unable to support life

deserts — the driest places on Earth, receiving less than 10 inches (25.4 cm) of rain per year

drought — a time when much less rain falls than usual, causing extreme dryness to the land

erosion — the wearing away of land by wind, water, and other forces

evaporate — to turn to vapor and vanish into the air

habitat — an environment where plants and animals live and grow

irrigate — to supply land with water using ditches or pipes

jojoba — a desert plant whose seed contains valuable oil

nomads — people who move from place to place looking for grazing land

nutrient — a substance needed for life and growth

overgrazing — heavy feeding by animal herds, resulting in plant destruction

topsoil — the fertile layer of soil on the surface of the ground

wasteland — barren, dry land that cannot support life

windbreak — a barrier that lessens the force of the wind

Index

Africa 8-9, 10-11, 13
Aral Sea 20-21

badger 26-27

cactus (cacti) 4, 26
cash crops 9, 14, 25
cold deserts 6
computers 25
contour plowing 18-19
cotton 9, 14, 21
COUNTRIES:
    Australia 26; Ethiopia
    17, 19; India 16-17;
    Mali 8-9, 11, 12-13;
    Niger 17; Nigeria 17;
    Somalia 17; Soviet
    Union 20-21; Tunisia
    10-11; Uganda 17;
    United States 4, 5,
    19, 26, 27
cows 8, 11, 14, 19
coyote 26-27
crested lark 26-27

deforestation (see trees)
desert fox 26-27
desert plants 4, 21, 26
desert temperatures 4, 6
desert tortoise 26-27
desert wildlife 4, 26-27
desertification 4, 8-9,
    10-11, 12-13, 14,
    16-17, 18
deserts (natural) 4, 6-7,
    8, 11, 21, 20, 21,
    26-27
diamondback
    rattlesnake 26-27

dirt bikes 26
drip irrigation 24-25
drought 4, 9, 11, 12-13,
    14, 18
Dust Bowl 9
dust storms 9

erosion 4-5, 8, 16, 17,
    18, 19
evaporation 22-23, 25

farming 4, 8, 9, 11, 14,
    17, 19, 21, 22-23,
    24-25, 26
foggy deserts 6

grasslands 8, 11, 14
Great Plains 9
green collared
    lizard 26-27

irrigation 21, 22-23,
    24-25, 26

jojoba 25

kangaroo rat 26-27

Middle East 11
mining 26
Monument Valley
    (U.S.) 4-5

national parks 26
nomads 11, 12
nuclear-bomb testing 26
nutrients 14, 17

overgrazing 8, 12, 18

peanut farming 9, 14
Phoenix, Arizona
    (U.S.) 27
pocket mouse 26-27
prairie dogs 26
pronghorn antelope
    26-27

rainfall and snowfall 4, 6,
    11, 12
refugee camps 14-15
rocky deserts 4

saguaro cactus 4
Sahel 9, 12-14
salt 20, 21, 22-23
sandy deserts 4
scorpion 26-27
sheep 8, 11
Sonoran Desert (U.S.)
    4, 26-27
starvation 14-15

topsoil 8, 17, 18-19
trees 8, 12, 16-17,
    18, 19
turkey vulture 26-27

United Nations 17

wasteland 4, 8
wells 12, 21, 22-23
windbreaks 16, 17